By

Christopher P. Fannybottom

Thunder Enlightening
PRESS

For Mom.

ISBN 978-0-9832491-8-4

Thunder Enlightening
PRESS

How to be a
GREAT
MOM

GREAT MOMS

laugh uncontrollably at **ALL** of your jokes.

Mothers
hold their
children's
hands for
a while...
their
hearts
forever.

GREAT MOMS

make sure their sons regularly wake up to the

HEAVENLY

smell of frying

BACON.

GREAT MOMS

if the aroma of bacon isn't enough to rouse their sons from slumber, add a melodious

"BREAKFAST, BO-WEEEEEZ!"

What a mother sings to the cradle goes all the way down to the coffin.

Henry Ward Beecher

GREAT MOMS make Saturday mornings special by making PANCAKES.

GREAT MOMS

teach
their son's
second grade

SUNDAY
SCHOOL

class.

Love
never
fails.
1 Corinthians
13:8

GREAT MOMS

know that
going on a

VENTURE

is an
amazing way
for a family to
spend a Saturday.

GREAT MOMS

allow you to believe that, when you have been a brat, the offensive child could not have been you. It must have been

TOM MASON.

You will find that as you look back upon your life that the moments when you have really lived are the moments when you have done things in the spirit of love.

Henry Drummond

GREAT MOMS

know how to characterize you as being a "BIRD" in such a way that you know that she feels like being a bird is a WONDERFUL way to be.

GREAT MOMS

help you grow accustomed to being called names like

"HONEY."

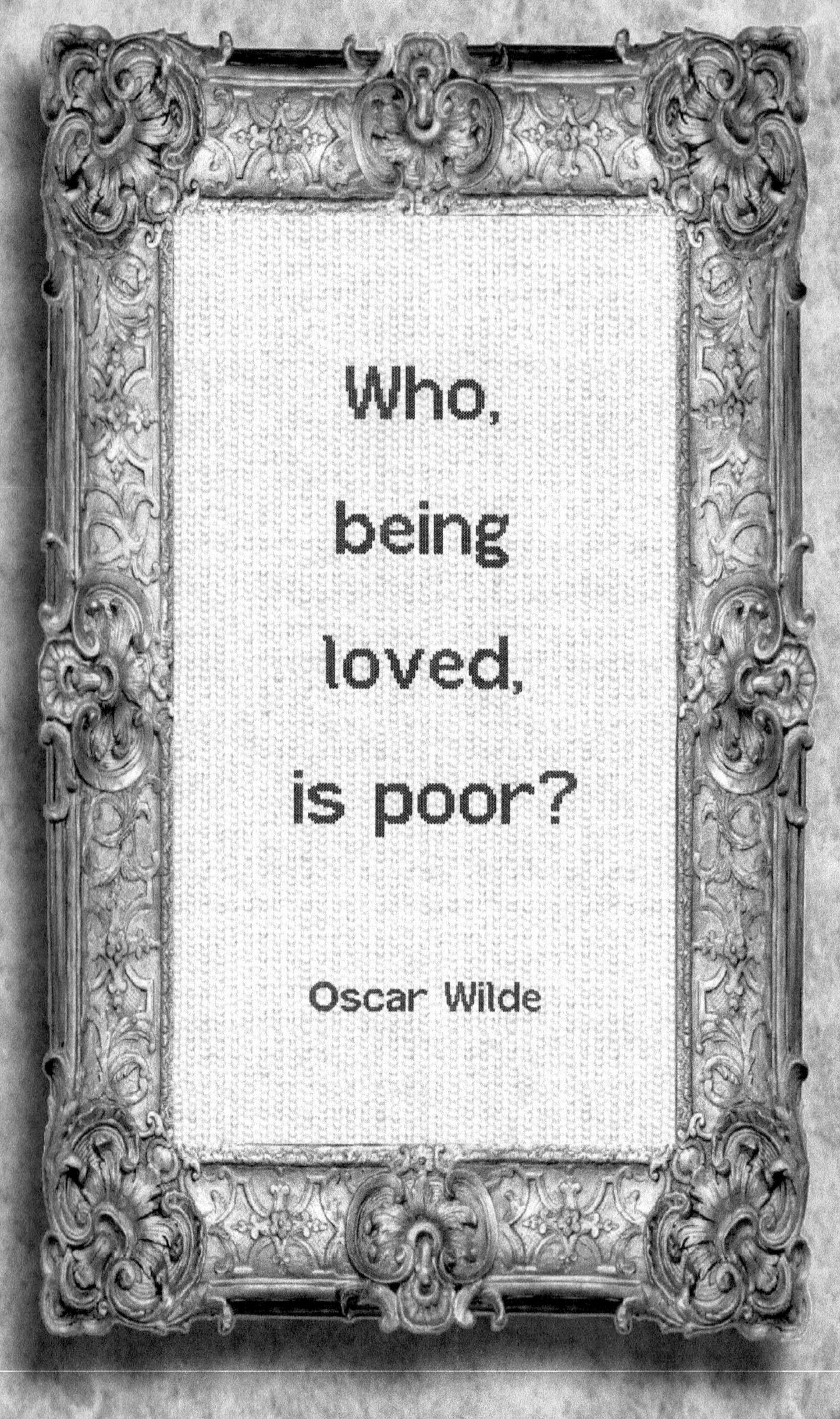
Who,
being
loved,
is poor?
Oscar Wilde

GREAT MOMS

help you learn to laugh at yourself by encouraging other names such as

"SPIT CURLS."

GREAT MOMS

buy their son
a book entitled
"YOU
Are Somebody
SPECIAL"
and give it to
him when he is
SEVENTEEN.

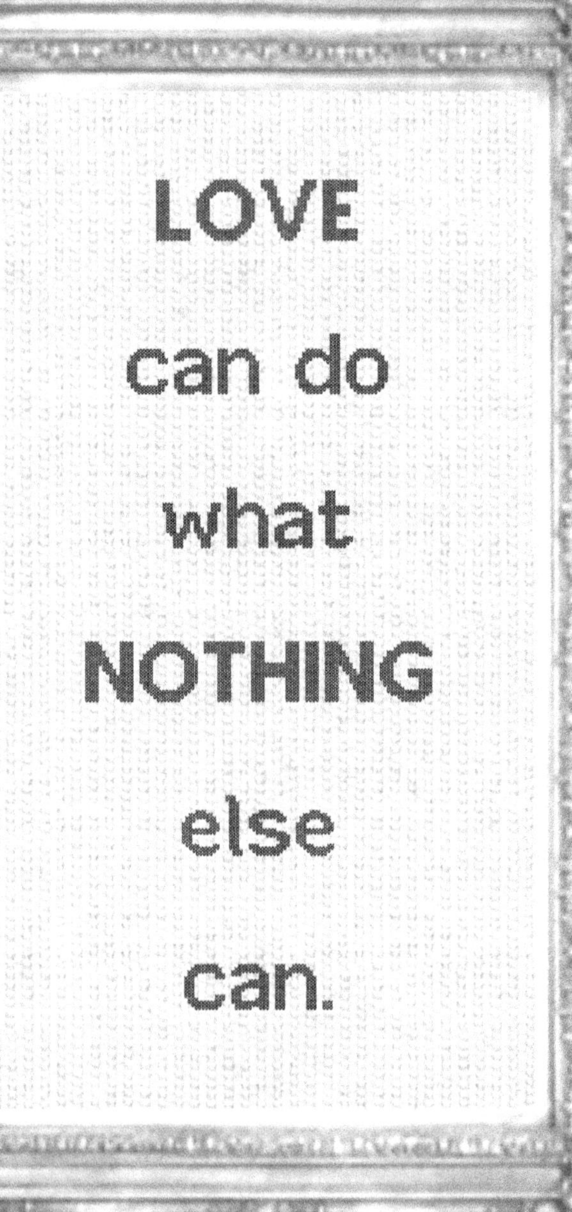
LOVE
can do
what
NOTHING
else
can.

GREAT MOMS

write things in the books they give their sons,

LiKE:

"With love to Chris, who is an inspiration," "To Chris, who already knows how special he is," and,

"Keep on spreading all that love around and you'll always be happy."

GREAT MOMS

have grateful sons who get

TEARY-EYED

when they read the things their Mom wrote in books twenty years ago.

As a mother comforts her child, so I will comfort you.

Isaiah 66:13

GREAT MOMS always make sure everyone has a STOCKiNG hung by the fireplace.

GREAT MOMS delight their families with fresh, home-made PECAN DIVINITY.

A
happy
family
is
but
an
earlier
heaven.

GREAT MOMS

freely forgive

ANYTHING

you may have done to defile her fresh, home-made pecan divinity.

GREAT MOMS would rather eat DOG FOOD DIVINITY before MISSING one of their son's games.

Every boy
who has
a dog

should also
have a
mother

so the dog
can be fed
regularly.

GREAT MOMS

buy you Christmas gifts no one else would because they know you in a way **NO ONE** else does.

(Who else would know how much joy a MUSICAL PHOTO PLANTER SUSAN would bring?)

Love ya' lots -
Anne

GREAT MOMS

make you feel like
Billy Graham,
Michelangelo,
Jim Thorpe,
Pavarotti or
Albert Einstein
depending on the

SITUATION.

M
is for
the
MANY
things you
gave me.

GREAT MOMS know how to mash one downright MEAN POTATO.

O
is for
the
OTHER
things you
gave me.

GREAT MOMS

love unconditionally, so there is

NO FEAR

in being her "open son."

T
is for
the
THOUSANDS
of things you
gave me.

GREAT MOMS

instigate great games like "Travel A.B.C.s," "Mad Libs," "Charades," and "QUESTIONS and ANSWERS."

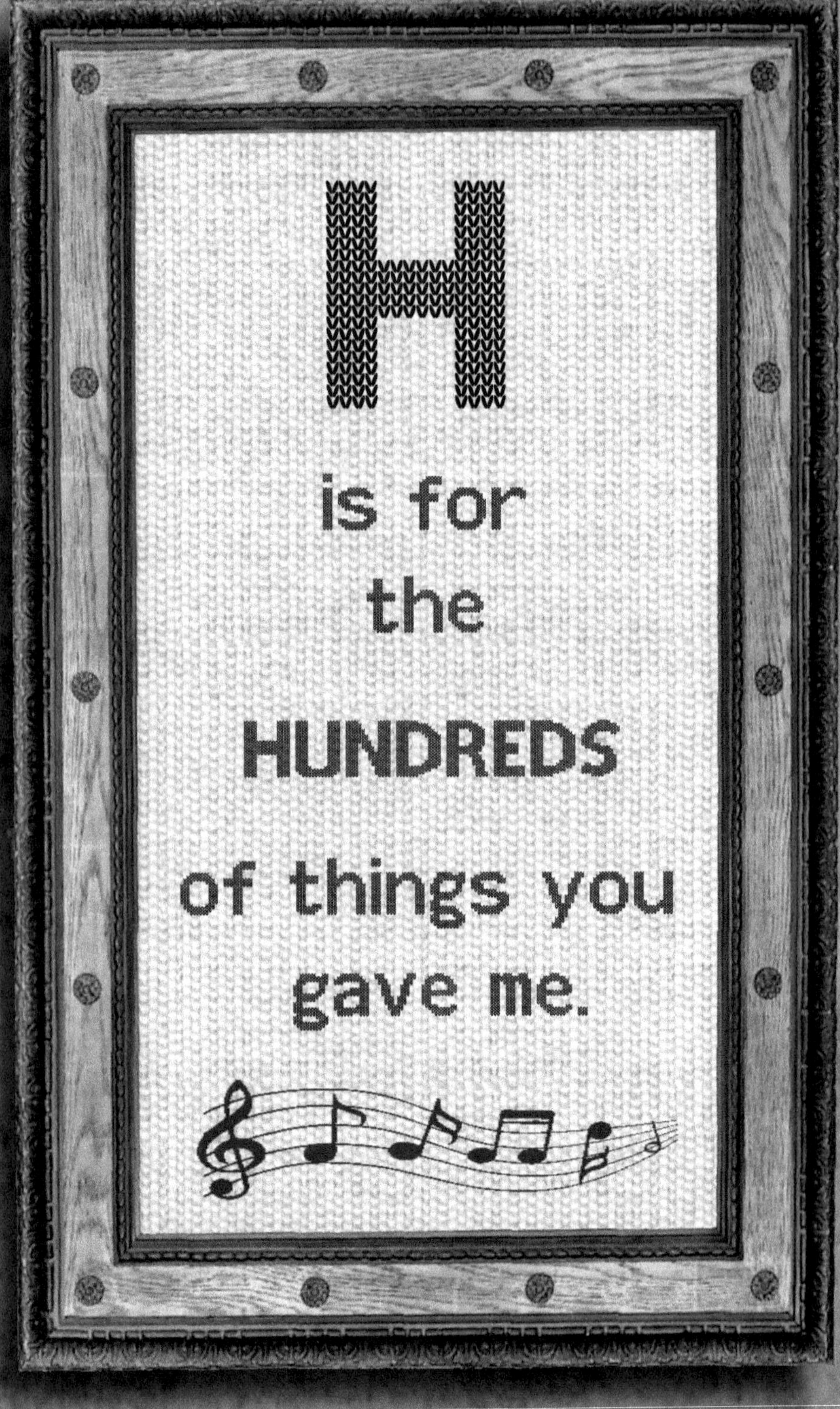
H
is for
the
HUNDREDS
of things you
gave me.

GREAT MOMS

will express great love for their son by knitting him a multicolored, patchwork

SWEATER VEST

when he is in the sixth grade.

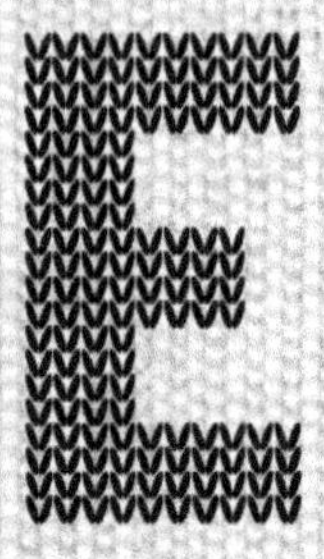

is

for

EVERYTHING

you

gave me.

GREAT MOMS

Will, in turn, be the recipients of a great expression of love when he turns around and, in front of all of his friends, actually wears the multicolored, patchwork

SWEATER VEST.

R
is for
the
REST
of the things
you gave me.

GREAT MOMS

love

GREAT DADS

with all their

HEARTS

which, in turn, is
a great blessing
to their sons.

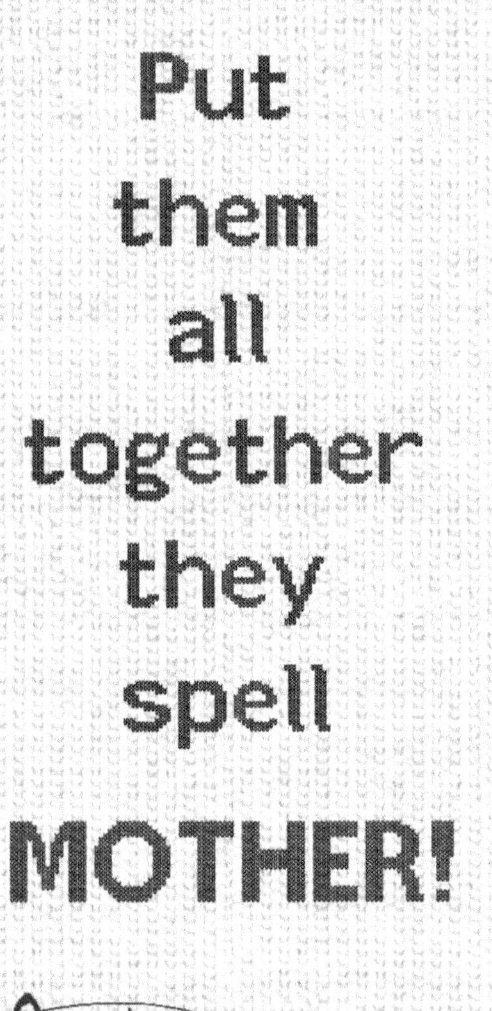
Put
them
all
together
they
spell
MOTHER!

GREAT MOMS hand-sew HALLOWEEN COSTUMES for their sons so they can pretend to be Batman and Robin.

If

a child

lives with

encouragement,

he learns

confidence.

Dorothy Law Nolte

GREAT MOMS

will always see
the beauty in the
slowly deteriorating
FELT SNOWMAN
Christmas ornament
you made as a
little boy.

GREAT MOMS

take years to demonstrate the qualities of a

GREAT WIFE

so their sons will know what to look for when the time comes.

GREAT MOMS freely embrace their DAUGHTERS-IN-LAW and love them like their own.

GREAT MOMS

grow up

to be

even

greater

GRANDMOMS.

SIX FLAGS

OLD NAV

GREAT MOMS make sure that their sons spend lots of time with MEMOMMIE and GANGIE.

GREAT MOMS

spend hours creating and mailing out

NEWSLETTERS

to her scattered brood that she wishes could spend more time together.

THE FAMILY

Rumble Report *Volume 12, Number 1* *January, 2002*

"A happy family is but an earlier heaven."

Remembering Christmas 2001

Christmas at the farm was a wonderful time for the family. Everyone was present except Nolan, who was in Gatlinburg with his basketball team, participating in a Christmas tournament. They were the champions, but Nolan was missed at the celebration.

Butch and Amy, Ty and Rita arrived late because Ty had a flat and a bad spare. Ty called Mom and Dad, who were on the road, too, and responded to the distress signal. The solution was a new set of tires for Ty and Rita--an unexpected Christmas gift for their car! When this was taken care of, they resumed their trip and were happily greeted upon arrival.

The weather was perfect, and outdoor activities were popular with the younger set. Everyone welcomed the new residents at the farm, the goat couple, Solomon and his wife (can't remember her name). The four-wheeler was in demand, as usual, with Matt and Angel, Chris and Cathy, Ty and Brad, and various children. Ty and Brad also tried out the rope swing at the treehouse.

The Grand Opening was highly entertaining, as it always is, and there was much laughing and admiring of gifts.

Finally, Family Christmas 2001 came to an end. Now we look forward to 2002, when we will meet at Butch and Amy's house for another Christmas to remember.

A New Year

(from one of Meena's old "expression" books)

He came to my desk with a quivering lip.
The lesson was done.
"Dear teacher, I want a new leaf," he said,
"I have spoiled this one."
I took the old leaf stained and blotted
And gave him a new one all unspotted
And into his sad eyes smiled,
"Do better now, my child."

I went to the throne with a quivering soul—
The old year was done.
"Dear Father, hast Thou a new year for me?
I have spoiled this one."
He took the old year, stained and blotted
And gave me a new one, all unspotted,
And into my sad heart smiled,
"Do better now, my child."

Papa and Meena's New Year's Eve Celebration

What Did You Like Best About the Rumble Christmas?

Butch and Amy: As always, we most enjoyed just being together, although we very much missed Nolan. Although we are so thankful for the gifts we received, the time together is much more important than the material gifts, and we know everyone else feels the same. The older we get, the more we feel that way. We are already looking forward to hosting our get-together next year, and we pray that we can find a day when everyone can be there. If not, we will still rejoice in the goodness of God to our family, and will be grateful for any time we can share together all year round. We love you all.

Brad: Four-wheeling around the farm and trying to avoid the cow patties.

Donna: Shrimp and Chick-fil-A nuggets! It was just fun giving and receiving gifts that were to "Donna and Brad."

Ty and Rita: We loved driving out to Hazy Hollow and spending time with the family. The house was decorated so beautifully and we love seeing all the cousins grow more and more every year. We think the way everything was done was perfect and the food could not have been better. We are so blessed with our family and we never want to take that for granted. We love everyone so much!

Ty: I enjoyed riding on that four-wheeler! There are only two things that I would want changed for next year:

1. I want Nolan to be there.
2. I don't want to catch another flat tire so that we have to run late and miss anything with the family.

Jason: The Rumble Christmas was fun, as usual. It couldn't get much better! I wish that more people would've had time to get some hot tub action! It was also a bummer that Nolan couldn't be there, but he couldn't help it.

Nolan: I always LOVE the Rumble Christmas, and would change nothing except for the fact that I would be there, and that I could see Matt's face when he got my gift!

Sarah Beth: What I liked best about Christmas was just having everybody there, with one exception. Whenever we can get the whole family together, it's just wonderful! I hate it that Nolan couldn't make it. I can't think of anything to make our Rumble Christmas better. It was perfect!

Chris: Spending time with Jason learning about E-bay and viewing the "Hardest job in America is being a Black Woman" T-shirt; reminiscing with my brothers; successfully riding the four-wheeler without getting cow dung all over me; playing Ty's new guitar (awesome); finally learning the official way to relieve myself in the woods (now I won't suffer the embarrassment of doing it wrong in the future); sharing the joy of all who gave and received crap holders.

Cathy: Seeing the excitement of the children.

Zachary: Going to the farm.

Kara: Being with the cousins and playing with my new book Meena and Papa gave me (Kid's Almanac).

Matt: The best thing about the Rumble Christmas was that Nolan wasn't there. :)

Angel: Christmas on the farm was wonderful (with the exception of missing Nolan). The decorations were beautiful, the food great, and, as usual, Meena outdid herself with her homemade gifts. I love hearing all the memories that Meena's gifts bring back to everyone.

Sierra: My favorite thing about Christmas was hanging out in Sarah Beth's room, playing with all my cousins and gifts.

Sydney: Loved seeing everyone but wondered "Where Nolie at?"

Ethan: Enjoyed tearing and rattling all the wrapping paper.

Papa: Being at the farm with all the family and seeing the result of a year's work by Meena.

Meena: I loved laughing together about the "olden days" and having Brad and Rita as official members of the family. I didn't care for the fact that Nolan wasn't there!

Moving Up the Ladder

Donna recently received a promotion at Lithonia Lighting. She is now a Marketing Specialist in Commercial Outdoor. She works for the Product Development manager of the General Purpose Outdoor products (this refers to the more economical stock and flow type products).

She works on a little bit of everything, from sales reporting of current market trends to assisting in many of the marketing efforts that come with new product introductions and project updates.

She is also assisting the department's Marketing Communications Specialist with product specification sheets. This task utilizes a lot of her desktop publishing skills.

In addition, she recently took a temp job at the Peach Bowl, and had a hand in making 12,000 Chick-fil-A sandwiches!

He had to get to the Shell station.

Chris' New Career

After much prayer and soul-searching, Chris has made a career change. Needless to say, his decision saddened the folks at Park Place Baptist. He is now account executive for Strategic Publishing, and will be working from home.

He also has incorporated a children's ministry, Future Hope, which targets 3rd - 8th grade children. He leads worship on Friday mornings at Edwards Middle School, and plans an event in January.

Before the holidays, he made the rounds from classroom to classroom as "The Reading Guitar Man," sharing a special Christmas program with the school children.

Added to his "good things" list is a Honda Odyssey which now is parked in his driveway and allows him to drive in style.

Happy Birthday, Butch!

February 15

In honor of Butch's birthday, the following is a poem written by Meena, and read at his "This Is Your Life" party on his 30th birthday. It commemorates a time when he was sent to his room as punishment. He was so indignant about this that he refused to speak to his mama, and instead walked to the door of her room and threw in a note.

When you were just a tiny boy,
And childhood was in bloom,
You sent to me a little note:
"Mike pee-peed in my room."

The punishment you had received- -
It must have seemed like doom
To make you want to write the words
"Mike pee-peed in my room."

You just refused to talk to me;
It was quiet as a tomb.
There was only one communique:
"Mike pee-peed in my room."

Your resentment was so plain to see.
You wore it like a plume
As you tossed that note in through the door- -
"Mike pee-peed in my room."

Many years have passed since then,
And now you are a groom,
But I remember just as plain
"Mike pee-peed in my room."

Sometimes when problems bother me
And there's an air of gloom,
These words are sure to bring a smile:
"Mike pee-peed in my room."

Giving Thanks

Thanksgiving this year was at Big Canoe, and the family (with the exception of Cathy and the newlywed couples) all gathered to spend time together.

Butch and Amy, Michael, Jackie, Jason, Nolan, Sarah Beth and Grant, and Papa and Meena sat down to a wonderful meal, provided by the ladies and Papa, who prepared the dressing.

Matt, Angel, Sierra, Sydney, and Ethan and Chris, Zachary, and Kara came later in the day, having had their Thanksgiving dinner elsewhere.

As usual, there was a lot of laughing going on, especially with a couple of new stories involving Matt. Everybody also enjoyed viewing the video which was shown at Ty and Rita's rehearsal dinner and listening to Chris read his book about Uncle Stinky.

The day ended with warm feelings and a wonderful anticipation of a Christmas celebration on December 22nd at the farm.

What's Happening With the Kids?

JASON

Jason ended the school term with a 3.5 GPA. Congratulations for that, and also for successfully scheduling his new classes so that he has a four-day-weekend every week!

NOLAN

Nolan's big news is his Christmas gift from Mom and Dad- - a black Jeep Cherokee Sport (same model as Papa and Meena's). Besides that, he ended a rewarding football season by earning the special teams award for his play. He was also the second scholar-athlete, with a 3.87 GPA. As noted elsewhere, his varsity basketball team won its Christmas tournament, and he recently scored 13 points in a JV game. A late news flash: he recently started a varsity game!

SARAH BETH

Sarah Beth closed out the volleyball season by winning the defensive award, Her biggest news, though, is her Christmas gift - - a horse! He's a quarter horse named Cody, 15 1/2 hands high, and brown with a white face. Since Christmas, he has acquired a stable mate, a pretty filly named Gypsy Rose.

GRANT

Grant continues to excel in sports, and is getting playing time on the 7th grade basketball team. Not only that, he got playing time in an 8th grade game - - the first 6th grader at Cleveland Middle School to achieve this feat. He also racks up As on his report cards.

ZACHARY

Zachary has pretty much recovered from a broken toe which he got at a friend's birthday party. As for his birthday party, Chris made a special trip to Charlie's Trading Post, where the shirt reject bin he knew and loved still exists, and selected party wear for Zachary and his guests. The boys were attired in shirts that said (for example): "Muncie South Running Rebels—We Don't Believe In Defeat," "Shemando Warriors," "Kinniwick," and lots of "ladies"—"Lady Indians," "Lady Rebels," "Lady Hornets," "Lady Pirates," and "Lady Lakers." They wore their party garb when they went out to eat.

At school, Zachary was invited to be one of six on the sixth grade math team. They meet before school to prepare for a national competition. He has been moved into advanced pre-algebra and will be taking algebra in seventh grade for high school credit.

KARA

Kara had the lead role of Mrs. Claus in the second grade school play, "Santa's Star Search." In it, she had a beautiful solo that made her daddy cry. She also was the narrator for the children's musical presentation at Park Place Baptist, and played two Christmas carols in her very first piano recital.

SIERRA

Sierra's basketball team has a record of 4 wins and 1 loss, and she's an important player. The first game was her best, as she scored 13 points in a 21 - 18 win. She celebrated her 8th birthday with a P.E. party in the Pickens Elementary gym. She had lots of guests, including Papa and Meena, Uncle Butch and Aunt Amy, and Uncle Chris and Kara. As one of her gifts, she received tickets to the Britney Spears concert from Uncle!

SYDNEY

Sydney played a pivotal role in keeping her family together during a recent truck crisis. After breaking down in Cumming, Matt called Angel to come to his rescue. Various methods to start the truck were tried, and the atmosphere was becoming rather heated. When tempers got short, Sydney would defuse the situation by saying, "Oh my goodness!" Several attempts were made to get going by Matt pushing and Angel steering. In this effort, they passed the same American flag several times, and each time, Sydney broke into "God Bless America." She did a very good job of facilitating!

ETHAN

Ethan is the proud owner of two new teeth, and has almost mastered the art of crawling, after his first attempts moved him backward instead of forward (much to the amusement of Uncle Butch and Uncle Chris).

GREAT MOMS

store away
memories
the way others
would store
away

GOLD.

A mother is
a person who,
seeing there
are only
four pieces
of pie for
five people,

promptly
announces
she never did
care for pie.

GREAT MOMS grieve when you grow up and MOVE AWAY to Texas.

GREAT MOMS CELEBRATE UPROARIOUSLY every time you return home.

Love
never reasons,
but profusely
gives its all

– gives like
a thoughtless
prodigal –

and
trembles then
lest it has
done too little.

Hannah Moore

GREAT MOMS

go to each one of their sons and ask,

"HOW CAN I CHANGE?"

at age 75.

GREAT MOMS

go bananas every time you do the

GREAT TRiCK.

Train a
child in
the way he
should go,
and when
he is old
he will not
turn from it.
Proverbs
22:6

GREAT MOMS

always find
new ways to

HAVE FUN

like doing
Facebook Live and
getting on stage at
The Uncle Chris
Show.

GREAT MOMS

never

stop

MAKING

WISHES.

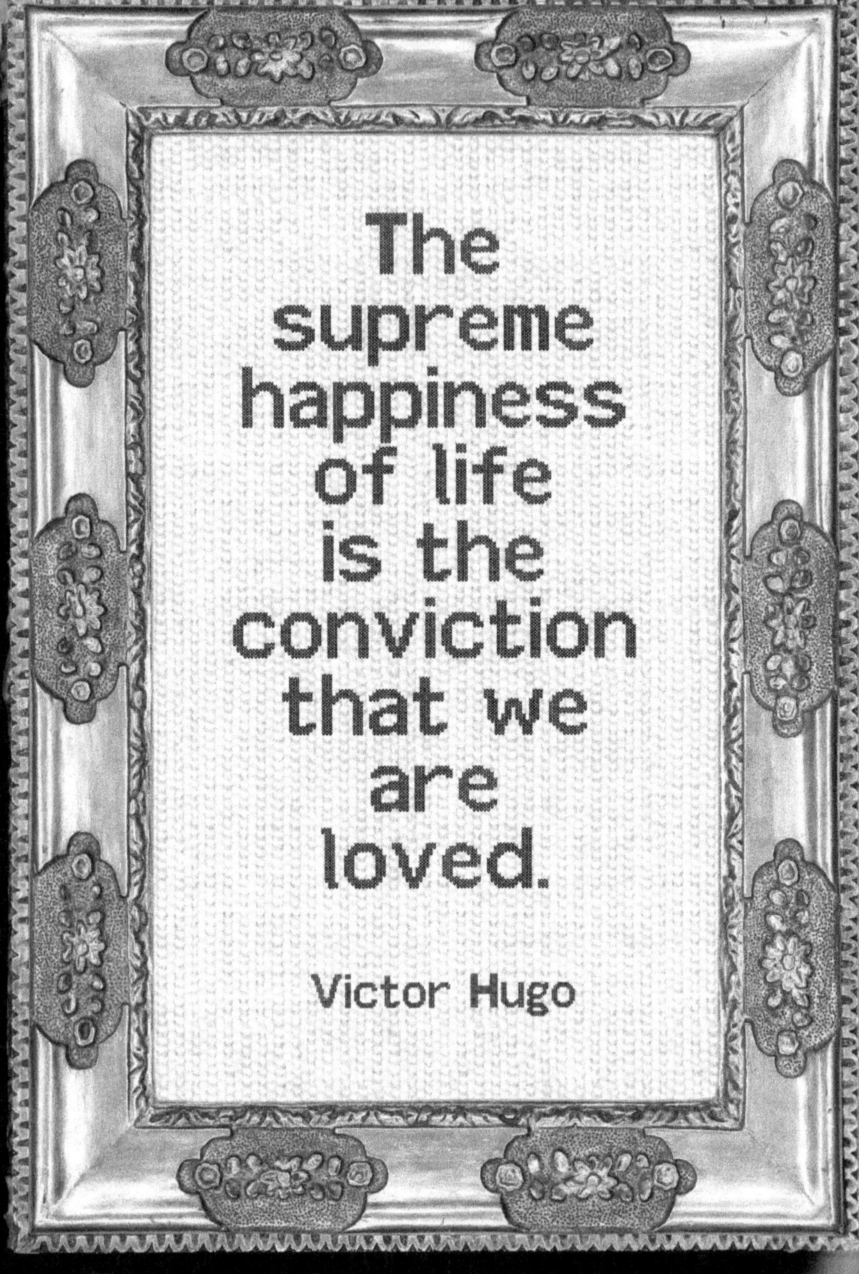
The
supreme
happiness
of life
is the
conviction
that we
are
loved.
Victor Hugo

GREAT MOMS

are always
Moms
but they
also become
a wonderful

FRIEND.

BY'S

www.ingramcontent.com/pod-product-compliance
Lightning Source LLC
LaVergne TN
LVHW010116170826
845678LV00012B/2430

* 9 7 8 0 9 8 3 2 4 9 1 8 4 *